This Notebook Belongs To

Made in the USA
Monee, IL
01 July 2021

72749850R00069